GOLD&
ASHES

By Feruza Afewerki

INTRODUCTION_

Gold & Ashes is a photo series that hopes to bring dignity and honour to the true stories of the Grenfell community. Creating this book has been a journey for me - one of discovering our resilience, connection and hope.

As the Grenfell tragedy unfolded, the mainstream rhetoric was filled with insensitive headlines and political talking points which seemed to never end. But there was another side to the tragedy, a far more important side about the lives of those who lived and loved in Grenfell Tower. The people who walked through the unimaginable and whose humanity, community spirit and strength held power.

Many have tried to dictate the narrative surrounding the Grenfell Tower tragedy and portray the community in a false light. Many have tried to speak for the lives lost in the tower, their families and friends without turning the lens to those very people. This is at the heart of what Gold & Ashes is - a space for Grenfell's humanity and stories of truth.

Seventy two lives were lost but each life was not just a number in a tragedy. That night, hundreds of families lost part of their world. I lost my big sister Amal Ahmedin and my three year old niece Amaya Tuccu-Ahmedin. Like many of the Grenfell residents, my sister and my niece were incredible human beings. As expected, my journey in creating this book was by no means easy. At times I was filled with deep grief and sorrow. In all honesty, there were moments where I wasn't sure if I could complete it, as each encounter magnified the loss we all felt. However, what came through more than anything on this journey was the resilience and inspiration of those featured in the book.

Gold & Ashes has been part of my personal healing process. It has enabled me to connect with others who understand and wish to see more done for the memories of their loved ones.

On top of the unbearable grief, the injustice has caused more hopelessness and anger. Despite everything, this beautiful, diverse and unified community has picked up the pieces and is rebuilding from the ruins with such dignity and love.

Their lives have inspired me to honour and document the memories of our loved ones. We as a community are different because of what we've walked through. But, we're still here - a living memorial of what was lost so that their lives are never forgotten. The depth of loss speaks to the depth of love we have experienced. We hold them in our hearts forever and are witnessing the legacy and imprint they have left on our lives.

This book features photo stories of the survivors, bereaved families and members of the local community, which I have compiled over the last two years. My artistic vision for Gold & Ashes was to simply share these stories authentically. The photography sessions were intimate and honest. We shared deeply vulnerable moments that will stay with me forever.

My hope is that this photo series will highlight the Grenfell community as they really are in their strength and dignity, reminding us that we are more than our trauma. I made the decision to introduce each contributor with their name instead of labelling them with titles like 'survivor' or 'bereaved'. I wanted to give those featured the chance to speak for themselves and tell their own story.

My hope for this book is that it humanises the Grenfell community - a community that I am proud to be part of and one which has held me through some of the most challenging periods of my life. This book is rooted in love, power and truth. May these stories at the very heart of Grenfell move you, provide you with insight and show the true courage of this community.

- Feruza Afewerki

DEDICATED TO_

This book is dedicated to Samia and Amaya, my driving forces for creating Gold & Ashes. To honour your lives, the light you were when living and in your death, your legacy of love and creativity is all over these pages.

To my father, your support from the beginning has meant everything. A freedom fighter at your core, Jigna. To honour who you have been all my life and for the pride in your eyes. Baba, your example has changed my life. You have taught me what it means to fight for freedom for myself and for my community. Losing you in this process has been the most difficult part.

The first people to move into Grenfell Tower in the 1970s experienced the luxury of new-build apartments. There was optimism in the air with the move to provide social housing to those who needed it most.

As time went on, the all-consuming push for new homes and the "right to buy" contributed to the decline of safe social housing provision in London. Where the local authority failed to maintain properties, the community advocated to improve living standards. Grenfell Tower was full of residents from different backgrounds, who all shared a strong sense of community.

In 2015 Grenfell Tower underwent a refurbishment as part of a local "regeneration" project in North Kensington. The choice of materials in this renovation was later found to be the primary cause of the rapid-fire spread in the 2017 Grenfell Tower fire. This included insulation made of a combustible plastic which released a combination of toxic gases when it burned. The ACM cladding chosen to improve the external appearance of Grenfell Tower was also flammable. The refurbishment was yet another example of cost saving being prioritised over residents' safety.

The Grenfell Action Group was formed in 2010 with a commitment to defend the rights of residents of Lancaster West Estate in West London. The Group's founding members, Ed Daffarn and Francis O'Connor, warned that "only a catastrophic event" resulting in the serious loss of life would bring an end to the "dangerous living conditions" in the block. Eight months after these words were written, the inevitable happened.

In the early hours of 14 June 2017, a fire broke out in Grenfell Tower. The materials chosen for the building refurbishment and the lack of regulations meant that the fire could not be contained and resulted in the deadliest fire in Britain since the Second World War.

Seventy-two innocent lives were lost and hundreds of residents were displaced.

The lives of the community surrounding Grenfell were forever changed.

ED DAFFARN_

"There is this kind of institutionalised indifference towards people living in social housing and Grenfell needs to be the catalyst for that change. It needs to be the point where you know, had we been listened to, had we been respected, had we been treated with some dignity Grenfell could have been avoided."

" I had my wonderful home and then you kind of open the door to a landing where I've got friendly faces and then into a community where I felt happy and into a wider community, Ladbroke Grove and Notting Hill, where I felt happy. The flats were built at a time when they really respected people. So we had this vast sitting room then a nice kitchen and separate bedroom, little bathroom and hallway that ran through it. It was full of light. I can't describe it, it just had a nice energy to it. "

"I hope we can find healing on an individual level. I am not personally bereaved. So for the bereaved, I hope they can find some peace and some healing. For the survivors, I hope they find a way of moving forward and be able to start a new life. But for all of us, I hope that we can get the justice and the change that needs to come as a result of seventy-two innocent people losing their lives."

THE RAGAB FAMILY_

" I miss his voice "

- Omar

"I miss his kindness, his kind heart, his generosity, everything. He was so kind and attentive to my needs."

- Shafika

"All my life, everything I did he was there. My wedding day he did my hair, in the hospital when I was in labour he was there. He's everything. All I can say is it's very painful...I lost my friend along with my brother in one go."
- Nashwa

In Loving Memory

Hesham Rahman   30 January 1960 - 14 June 2017

ZOË_

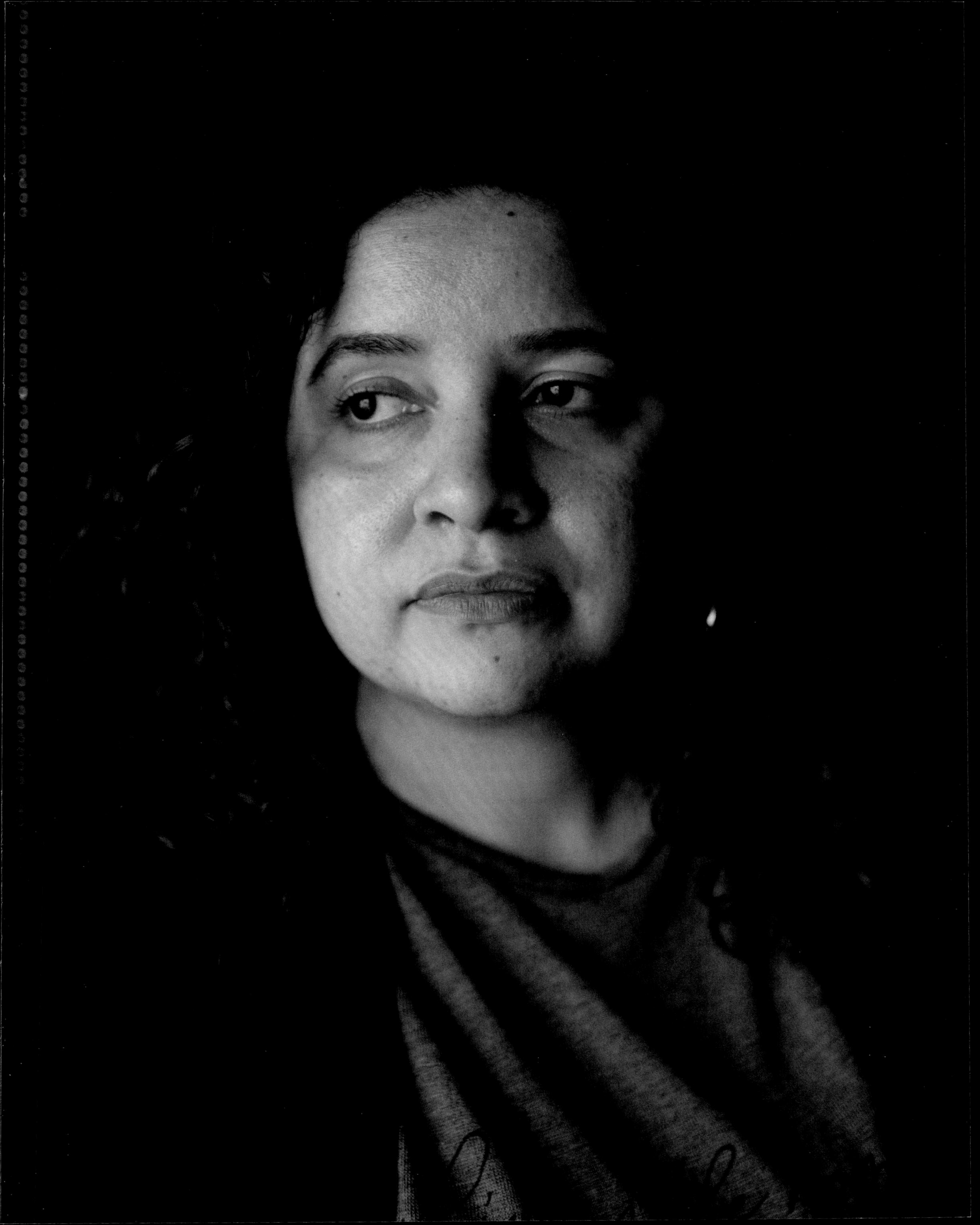

Sometimes you will be given what you wanted just to show you it is not at all what you needed.

I remember often walking past the homes that were just a stone's throw away from Grenfell witnessing "how the other half lived" – massive houses with high rise ceilings and huge windows, gates and fences, private parking spaces on their doorsteps and probably costing the same amount as a small private jet. The more I would walk towards home, the more the divide became apparent. High rise blocks, council estates, overcrowding and definitely not a gate or fence in sight. Even the street properties with three to four separate flats in them were worn out – you could tell which ones were home owners and which ones were social housing just by how they looked from the outside. I recall walking past the homes of how the other half lived and sometimes saying out loud "One day." Little did I know it would happen like this. I definitely do not live in anything close to the homes of how the other half live – but I have my own front door, doorstep and even my own doorbell.

Funny how one of the labels the government/council gave us when we lost our homes was "displaced." – because even though I am settled where I am now, a part of me still feels displaced.

It is a bitter sweet feeling. There is almost a feeling of selfishness. Ungrateful almost. My home was replaceable - but the lives of the loved ones we lost are not. The comments outsiders looking in have made infuriates me – we have been called things like 'privileged' and 'lucky' and that we get "special treatment". They nearly killed us, they killed our loved ones and completely destroyed us – what part of that is privileged and lucky? This was much more than losing the place I called home – I, like many others, lost myself. We lost innocent friends, neighbours and loved ones because those who had a duty to us did not care enough to ensure our safety was their priority. There was no "special treatment" – it was the opposite. While there have been some achievements and progress, equally there are still obstacles and battles we have to fight just to be heard and for action to be taken - there is still no "special treatment" and even if there is a fraction of it, it feels as if it is too little, too late.

But we will continue to do what we can to ensure the safety of others is a priority.

It has been 1000 days since we went to sleep at night and tragically, that was the last time our loved ones laid their heads down to rest. It has been 1000 days since our normal came to an end. It has been 1000 days since our community came together and also fell apart. It has been 1000 days since many of us had a good nights sleep. It has been 1000 days since we smiled genuine smiles and laughed genuine laughs.

It has been 1000 days since our lives changed forever – and I would happily say goodbye to what I wished for 1000 times over if it meant we could have our 72 loved ones back with us and none of this ever happened.

1000 days. 72 loved ones. Forever In Our Hearts.

By Zoë Dainton - Grenfell Tower Resident

ROSIE & ANDREIA_

"We've lived around here a long time and I've always loved this area...but it just feels different now. People are more at ease with each other because everybody now shares the same experience so that does something...in like a positive way, just that closeness."

- Andreia

"I really miss Fethia. I wish she was here now...she was my best, best, best friend, I'm sad that she died, a lot."

- Rosie

In Loving Memory

Fethia Hassan   5 October 2012 - 14 June 2017

Hania Hassan   4 June 2014 - 14 June 2017

LUCY_

SUSAN_

"I think there was still smoke coming out the building at that point and yet this huge amount of determination to try (and no one could make it better) but to try and make the best of a situation and to come and try and help in any way that people could and that, that was incredibly powerful...I'd never seen community coming together on that sort of scale."

"What became important was that before the fire there was very much that thing about people's voices not being heard. But there is that history in the community about fighting for spaces and taking back spaces that I've grown up with."

- Lucy

"The trauma was just completely everywhere, wherever there was people. The bus driver was affected, the shopkeeper was affected, you know, obviously not the same effect of the next of kin and very close losses, but you know the people in the street all the adults in the street were crying and sobbing and there was an outpouring of grief and loss everywhere. So for the children and adolescents they were witnessing people that they relied upon struggling. Mothers and fathers and teachers and whoever. So for them to have a space which they could own and have, that they could process their feelings and thoughts into in trusted spaces with trusted outsiders, art psychotherapists that came in to respond, was very important."

- Susan

LEANNE & MALACHI_

"You accumulate so much pain over the years and you look at what the council can do, these people are supposed to be human beings so in my head it's just like there is no good left....but that night was amazing, when I finished Grace for Grenfell I just remember thinking, wow, people are beautiful, people can be beautiful."

- Leanne

"I had this guilt in my stomach of not being able to do more and it was always replaying in my mind exactly how everything went that night...one of the things that came to me was, at the time I was in the wheelchair and every step you take, whether it's an actual physical step or a step in your mind, you're progressing, not regressing."

- Leanne

NATASHA_

"In September 2017, I decided to join the committee and come and help fight and try and change the narrative around what Grenfell was about, to try and create some sort of legacy... my driving force is to ensure it never happens again.

As a mother of three children, for me personally it's the children. We lost one too many, eighteen is way too many to lose. They never had an opportunity to live a life, and that's what makes me get up in the morning. When days are tough, and there are tough days in this process, I've got to remember, you know, that there were so many children that never had a chance to experience life. I lost my uncle and he will always be the reason I do this. But I do also say he lived a bit of a life, it was cut short, but adults tend to live a life. You know when you're an adult, you see and do things that children that are not even born yet, never would have, never had an opportunity to. For me that's what hurts the most. That thought will continue. When things are not going our way, I'll just remember those children and continue to push forward for it to never happen to anyone else."

GABY & ESTHER_

"We as a family also found it all tough, everybody was affected by it. As a mum, I was trying to make sure the children were all okay and not really knowing how to do that.

When you've lost everything in front of you. You know when you feel like as a community you haven't got much else to lose - something like this happens to you, you don't feel like...there are things worth fighting for. And perhaps before we didn't feel like there were things worth fighting for quite so hard and I think it motivated a lot of people to do things they wouldn't have done. I think to have that kind of experience which draws people together is really precious, there is something really precious about it. It is totally tragic, really horrendous you wouldn't want it to happen to anyone again but there is gold that can be redeemed by it."

- Gaby

"I think the best kind of memorial in a way is a memorial that can change lives and change laws and change practice, where there were so many things that can go wrong in this situation. I think that's the kind of memorial that will be fitting so that other people would not have to go through what they went through. I think that would be fitting. Like a living memorial.... That's partly why I wrote Grenfell Hope. I don't want people to forget or to feel powerless. I want people to know that they can do things and we each can make a difference."

- Gaby

Feruza: Esther, how do you think
Amaya wants to be remembered?
Esther: "In a nice way"

In Loving Memory

Amaya Tuccu-Ahmedin   25 February 2014 - 14 June 2017

MOUNA_

" I've lost confidence within myself. Being with Grenfell United and people that could literally bring back the confidence in you. I think being surrounded by good people really does help. "

“We had a park downstairs where our children will play together. You know you can just leave your children with your neighbour and they will look after them and watch them until you come back.”

FERUZA_

Photography by Tara Leigh

"Growing up, I wanted to be just like her. She was the life of the party, she would dance her heart out, the light that shone brightest in every room. So much energy, generosity and above all love. I remember stealing her clothes and hiding her make up every chance I got. We called her Samia, and she was my big sister, always looking out for me, always wanting me to have fun and do well in whatever I pursued. Never one to hold grudges, she wanted the absolute best for those around her and she showed me how to live life to the full.

She spoke six languages and her door was always open, she loved people well and because of this she was always making friends. I still want to be like her and this book is part of her legacy. Her example showed me how to reach out to those in your community, sit down over coffee and connect because no matter who you are or where you come from, we all have our humanity in common."

In Loving Memory

Amal Ahmedin   1 January 1982 - 14 June 2017

Amaya Tuccu-Ahmedin   25 February 2014 - 14 June 2017

CORINNE_

"I really enjoyed the space because we was above the ground, just felt like we was in the clouds away from all the hustle and bustle of life. The views were amazing. Didn't matter what time of the night it was, there was motion. There were cars on the dual carriageway you could see somebody walking, so there was lots of things to look at no matter what time of the day it was and I always loved that about Grenfell. I loved the sunsets as well, because where my front room was, the sun would be coming down in the area...if you spoke to my children they would be like, "Mummy was always taking pictures of the sunset and the different colours." So that was something I really, really enjoyed about living in Grenfell. I would chart where the sun would set in summer time and in winter time and on the 21st of June, the longest day.

I was really looking forward to seeing how far the sun would go to the right when it was setting but I obviously didn't get to have that opportunity because the fire took place on the 14th which was a few days before that."

"I remember just thanking my oldest son saying just 'thank you for waking up, thank you for waking me up'."

"Both my children were in shock. My oldest, his eyes were just open wide for like twenty four hours. I could see that he was in a state of shock and I was concerned just about how it would affect the children going forward. Their primary school was five minutes from Grenfell and from their playground you could see the Tower and I didn't want them to go to school, I just wanted them to be close to me."

TURUFAT_

" It's tough for our community because, especially in this tragedy there is no conclusion "

"How beautiful a community
we were....everyone was living
a normal life, just a beautiful
community. Living there for
more than 20 years, I never
had any problem, I never had
any single worry, for me living
there, even after I had Abem,
so happy, so grateful."

TIAGO_

"For Grenfell United our sense of justice is, and there are many strands of it: personal, criminal, proceedings and second of all, the enquiry coming out with good recommendations to ensure that it never happens again.

There have been many fires that have happened since the tower. Fortunately no one has died but it's going to continue to happen until someone doesn't allow it. If we're not going to hold these people to account then no one will."

BOBBY ROSS_

REST IN POWER

1953–2017

"At the time I couldn't see the blessings because obviously I've lost my dad in a fire, I've lost my home, I lost everything. But I didn't see the blessings that were around like my partner, the volunteers that were helping and they've stuck by me all up until now.

I literally found my purpose is helping people through their situation. It's more amazing when you know that you've helped someone get from the lowest point where they're at and now they're starting to see a future. Before people would say "I can't see a future, I don't know where I'm going. It's all bleak" and when you hear that same person come back to you and say "I can start to think see things now clearly". "

"How would I describe him? Hmm, there are so much words I can say. He was an activist for Grenfell. He'd always look out for the underdog, it didn't matter where you was from, what colour your skin was and he was a white Irish man. He'd go all out to help that person's situation and then he'd feel good, you know what, yeah I've got them, I've told the council about this, that. I have changed this, that. Like the prayer room for instance, I'm that thinking - you're Irish, you're not even Muslim, what are you doing? But he didn't care, it was the fact that he was defending people who weren't able to speak for themselves or the fact that they're not listened to. He was very community-orientated. He loved his community, he was always out and about in the community."

In Loving Memory

Steve Power   18 August 1953 - 14 June 2017

THE MUSSILHY FAMILY_

"At that time I didn't really know how to express my emotions with words right, so with him, he put his arm around me and that said a million things. Or he would just say a sentence. "Don't worry Karim, everything is going to be alright". Something along those lines.

I remember he was quite hard on us, in a good way because he didn't say it directly but everyone would tell us how much he cared for us and as the years went on, I found out more and more and more. I just wish I spent more time with him. I didn't spend as much time as I know he would have liked."

- Karim

"You had a life before Grenfell and you have a life after Grenfell and they're two completely different things. I feel like it will never be the same. Not because of losing Uncle Hesham but how we lost him. So publicly, so horrific and everything that came with it. The impact has filtered down, not just for myself, my nan, my uncle or Noha, or my brother and my sister, you know. To all of us, to my kids, to the point where it impacted all of our lives in a way where things will never be the same again. I've got my kids asking me questions I don't know how to answer. Questions that kids shouldn't be asking. Put in situations where you only thought it existed in movies. I don't have words for the impact because I feel like it's still happening, it's still progressing and it's not getting better, it's getting worse. People say time heals but in this case I feel like we're not able to start the process of moving on until there is some type of closure. The impact has been unimaginable. I never expected anything like this to happen to us or that by trying to do the right thing by his name was going to have such a negative impact as well.

Losing anybody is tough. Everytime we think about it, you get so angry. You have this anger concealed inside of you and you don't know where to project this anger and that's scary and you start worrying, are you going to be projecting it in the wrong ways? I feel trapped in this emotional sort of place with these negative emotions because there's no closure and it feels like no one is really trying to do anything about that apart from us. And that's why it's frustrating because it always feels like if we don't try to do something, justice, whatever that looks like, nothing is going to happen. I can't move on knowing that my family was killed in this way and accept that. You're given some support and therapy and told off you go back into the world, I can't accept that. There's a lot of people that feel the same as me.

But I guess that's what keeps us going, knowing that our families are being remembered for this culture of neglect and greed and we can't allow that to stay the same. We will continue to fight until some positive changes come from this and this never happens to anyone else."

- Karim

In Loving Memory

Hesham Rahman   30 January 1960 - 14 June 2017

DAVID_

"Music has been one of things that has helped me get through. If I can
be one of the ones that care and do my little bit to make a change then
that's the most important thing for me."

TIM_

"When you realise that because of where you live, or because of social economic factors, all the things that you have been told by those in authority are at best just plain lies. You are told to put your trust in the government and officials as they have your best interests, and it turns out to be absolute nonsense. There's one rule for them, and there's one rule for us. Well we can do this but you can't do that, because we make the rules and you don't, you stay there, and don't make a fuss, because if you make a fuss we can make your life very difficult."

"That's what being human is. If you see someone in trouble you help them. You must have empathy for people, you can't just stand by and say "Well, probably your fault". Humans help humans, that's how society works. You learn, you understand, you talk and discuss, and that's how you move forward. So when you see someone in pain, you don't just go 'that's not my business', especially when it's on your doorstep. You don't do that, you run to it and you help, you try and do what you can, surely that's what people do, try and help."

ZEYAD_

"Once those first 48 hours cleared and the authorities were nowhere to be seen, I decided there's no chance I'm leaving the community right now like this. There's no way. I told my manager I'm not coming back until I feel like there's something happening here, I'm not coming back...I ended up leaving my job, I was there for five years you know, so yeah I left them. Something needed to be done and I believed that's what community is for, to be strong for those who couldn't be."

"For me personally, I genuinely love this place. It's not just because I've grown up here and all my friends and stuff were here, I think it's more like, well just the community here before Grenfell. It's home, there's no better feeling, I found myself coming out of the train at Ladbroke Grove Station and like I'm smiling because I dunno, I just feel something in my soul, like rah."

"I believe in the silence and I believe in what it does for our community that's why I lead it. The silence makes us inclusive to everyone, to children to the eldest of elders. It's not aggressive, it's not violent, we're not on the blink of riots. It's a time to be conscious get your emotions out, take some time to think."

SWARZY_

"Letting people tell their story has always been part of our history. It has always been part of activism or it's always been part of change. And yeah, if you don't tell your story, the danger is that someone else might tell it for you."

"What I learnt as part of the Good News of Jesus Christ is that people are made in the image of God which means people are made whole with dignity and value and love, and all of that is intact. So the minute anything comes to war against this truth, you must stand up. You must stand up and say that's wrong. You must stand up for people who may not even have their own voice or strength to stand up for themselves."

" Khadija was one of my closest friends but she was also everyone's closest friend. She was just an amazing person to have around. "

"So I met Khadija at secondary school, and that's where I guess we formed our friendship. Our friendship group was comprised of me and maybe about four other friends, and we were all just quite, I don't know, silly at times, fun, nice sometimes. But Khadija was always the voice of reason but in the nicest way and she was very grounding as a person. So if you were having troubles and you were talking to her about it, when she spoke to you she would make you see how maybe futile it was. She was lovely, she was such a lovely person.

I never heard her speak badly about anybody, honestly. Everybody goes through their little bitchy phase in school, but she never seemed to have that. She always seemed to be quite secure in herself. But also her mum was really loving and really, really kind and she was a reflection of her mum too. A lot of love had been put into Khadija from her Mum."

In Loving Memory

Khadija Saye   30 July 1992 - 14 June 2017

Mary Ajaoi Augustus Mendy   11 June 1963 - 14 June 2017

ADIAM_

"We had plans for our children, when they grew up together...all our dreams are gone."

- Adiam

"She was my everything, she was more than a friend. She was my sister, my best friend. No one is like her, no one can replace her. From morning to night we would just be laughing and having fun, we didn't even have to talk, she would give me a look and we would just laugh."

In Loving Memory

Amal Ahmedin   1 January 1982 - 14 June 2017

Amaya Tuccu-Ahmedin   25 February 2014 - 14 June 2017

SUE & MAXINE_

"I only knew Amaya and her parents - they were a family at my nursery. She was a little girl I looked after for nearly two years everyday. So for me, it's just heartbreaking that such a small life can be snatched away so cruelly."

 - Sue

BELLAL_

"My daughter, at the time was eleven going on twelve. My son was seven and my other daughter was three. So I had three kids and my wife was five months pregnant.

I'm speaking to my family on the phone but I'm also watching it on TV simultaneously. I'm someone that you ask me something I could tell you, "I think this and I think that." But that night, I didn't think anything. I didn't know what to say. Initially, I told them to leave the flat. They couldn't, the hallway was full of thick black smoke. She couldn't see past the handle. So now I'm in a predicament where, she's telling me, she can't leave but it looks worse outside than it sounds inside.

I can see on the TV that the fire is spreading from the outside so it's getting bad. So I was in a dilemma where do I tell her to go or do I tell her to wait. The fire services are saying they're coming but they're taking long and it's not looking promising."

"Just to give you an insight into my thought process or my prayer at that time was, "O Allah, I just want one of them to survive" because asking for all four at the time felt a little bit selfish or shall I say four and a half, especially with the condition of the Tower.

I think coming to that stage of not knowing what to say and not knowing what to do, I think that stage is probably the most humbling stage of my life. It humbles you, because what it then shows you is, well actually, you think you know answers to everything but you don't.

Here you are with your family asking you what to do and you don't have an answer. Because you tell them to leave and something happens to them you're gonna live with that guilt. Tell them to stay and something happens to them, you're still gonna live with that guilt."

"For days if not weeks after the fire, my family's condition was still unknown except for my youngest and obviously it plays on your mind. Like, has my prayer come true? Is she going to be the only one that's going to survive? Thankfully that was not the case and they all survived."

JOSEPH JOHN_

"I still feel like I'm living back in 2017 to be honest, mentally. I still get flashbacks, I'm not really eating or sleeping properly. I'm still trying to cope day to day. There's no time frame on our mental health, after seeing what we've seen, after surviving, after going through the smoke. People have been going through a lot. You can't put a time on that. We are still healing. It hasn't been an easy road from 2017."

THE BERNARD FAMILY_

"My brother Raymond AKA Moses was just a very calm-natured man. He loved his family. He would not only put himself out for his entire family but for anyone whom he felt he had a relationship or bond with. In fact Moses would help complete strangers. The loss of Moses in our family is massive, he was my rock and the rock that held the family together in the UK. Our parents emigrated back to Trinidad in the 80s. However, Moses and I made the decision to remain in the UK and from that point onwards, Moses became the head of our family unit in the UK."

- Bernadette

" Moses was a father figure to all my children and grandchildren. He played a vital

role in the decisions I made in raising them. Moses laughed with them, played with

them, held them when they were sad and needed reassurance and he was, and remains

in memory, an inspiration to all my children and grandchildren. "

- Bernadette

"He's very selfless, probably the most selfless person you've ever come across... you would always see him smiling, joking, always around."

- Sarah-Jayne

Raymond AKA Moses Bernard (My Uncle Moses)

My Hero, my confidante.

The only man in whom I put my Trust.

I lost him on that fatal night as I stood and watched the bright burning light.

Just a couple of hours before the flames, we had made plans
for the next day, to do, what we would usually do, nothing special, just spend
time together, joking and laughing.

But, instead, what I did was watch the flames rise higher and higher until it
engulfed the Tower, there was nothing I could do to save my Hero, my Uncle
Moses.

All I could do was to stand and watch, crying, screaming in pain.

I spent days crying near the Tower, looking for my Uncle, hoping in vain, that
just maybe, just maybe, he was on the streets, lost but alive.

My memories of my Uncle Moses, sometimes make me cry, the way he
protected me, the way he tried to protect other families, his laughter and the joy
of just being around him.

My Uncle Moses, a generous man with the biggest heart.
He was gentle, funny to say the least, but most of all he was kind beyond belief.

Nothing was ever too much for him to do for me or other
people in his life, he always made time for everyone.

He was charming, he was suave with (as the saying goes) a heart of gold, always
helping people to try and reach their goals.

His house was open to all his neighbours, all of whom he made welcome, all to
whom he showed love and understanding.

My perfect Angel, My Uncle, Raymond AKA Moses Bernard.

By Zoe-Ann Bernard-Panton, Niece

WRITTEN ENTRY- DEDICATION

In Loving Memory

Raymond 'Moses' Bernard   22 May 1954 - 14 June 2017

The El-Wahabi Orchard

Let us remember those who died in the tragedy of the Grenfell fire.

Let us remember and not forget.

Let us remember, united in grief, and hope and love.

Abdulaziz   Faouzia
El-Wahabi   El-Wahabi
52 years   42 years

Yasin   Nur Huda   Mehdi
El-Wahabi   El-Wahabi   El-Wahabi
20 years   15 years   8 years

THE WAHABI FAMILY_

"My brother was great - he was like a dad to be quite honest. He was very British in many ways and also held onto a lot of Moroccan cultures as well, so if you went to his place you would see like a lot of Moroccan artefacts and stuff that he would bring back. He did like boats, like fisherman boats and would have some of their models in his house. He was a hands-on dad and would go to all the parent meetings and things like that and very supportive of me. I am the youngest in the family, so I was the baby sister kind of thing. He loved my mum and my mum loved him. That's my brother, a very great dad, great brother, great son. Faouzia was really good at cultural foods, she taught me how to cook many Moroccan dishes and she would also try other dishes. We used to bake sometimes. I'd go upstairs to their flat, we'd bake together and sometimes we tried different recipes from books. She loved to sew, she used to teach my daughter every week. We used to have dinner and every week she showed Sara how to knit. She used to go to a knitting club and they used to sew baby outfits and baby socks. She used to sell them with my youngest, Sara, on Portobello together and then they used to give whatever they made to charity. She was very involved with the community. Yasin was the eldest, he was a really good brother to his siblings, really caring, always happy, always smiling, always helping people with shopping. Like he'll see people coming into the block and he'll help them with their shopping and kind of thing. My eldest nephew Yasin was 20 years old, Nur Huda was 15 and my son Zak who was 16 at the time was very close to them. My daughter Sara was very close with her cousin Mehdi and they were both 8 at the time."

- Hanan

" I think, obviously being a survivor was the most difficult aspect in my life. However, I do feel honoured and privileged that I knew these people and that I actually lived within the Tower. The way people visualise what it's like to live in a tower block, you kinda think everyone keeps themselves to themselves and noone knows anybody and there's not many positive thoughts. When actually, it's a real community because you're so close knit and you do support each other. I just felt like people in that Tower just cared so much for each other whether they knew you personally or not. "

- Hanan

" Yasin was always a supportive figure in the lives of his young cousins like me and in the community. He was a sociable and popular person. He would always help neighbours with their bags and open doors. I felt inspired by his drive to create a better life for himself and his family. I will always strive to be as social and as outgoing as him, so that a piece of him can live on through me. "

- Zak

Has it really been four years since the day some of us escaped?

Has it really been four years since the memories that I have taped?

Has it really been four years since my heart began to ache?

Has it really been four years since my soul began to break?

Goodbye to my family.

Goodbye to my friends.

Goodbye to my neighbours.

Goodbye to my home.

Has it really been four years since the day of the screams?

Has it really been four years since the visions of extremes?

Has it really been four years since 72 people were snatched away?

Has it really been four years since we thought we were all here to stay?

The 14th June was when we thought they were going to follow.

The 14th June was when we all began to feel hollow.

The 14th June was when the community felt the pain.

The 14th June was when the memories became a stain.

Has it really been four years since the banging on the windows could be heard?

Has it really been four years since the community came out in herds?

Has it really been four years since we all began to pray?

Has it really been four years since we wished our loved ones could have stayed?

Imagine if we could turn back time and undo the suffering.

Imagine if we could turn back time and take away the bustling.

Imagine if we could turn back time and did not have to pretend.

Imagine if we could turn back time and take away their end.

Has it really been four years since we could hear your laughter?

Has it really been four years since 72 of you went to the hereafter?

Has it really been four years since the vivid memories etched on my mind?

Has it really been four years since it became clear that rules need to be refined?

Has it really been four years since questions are still unanswered?

Forever in our hearts.

Sara Chebiouni - Bereaved and Grenfell Tower Resident

The El-Wahabi Orchard

Let us remember those who died in the
tragedy of the Grenfell fire.

Let us remember and not forget.

Let us remember, united in grief, and
hope and love.

Abdulaziz
El-Wahabi
52 years

Faouzia
El-Wahabi
42 years

Yasin
El-Wahabi
20 years

Nur Huda
El-Wahabi
15 years

Mehdi
El-Wahabi
8 years

In Loving Memory

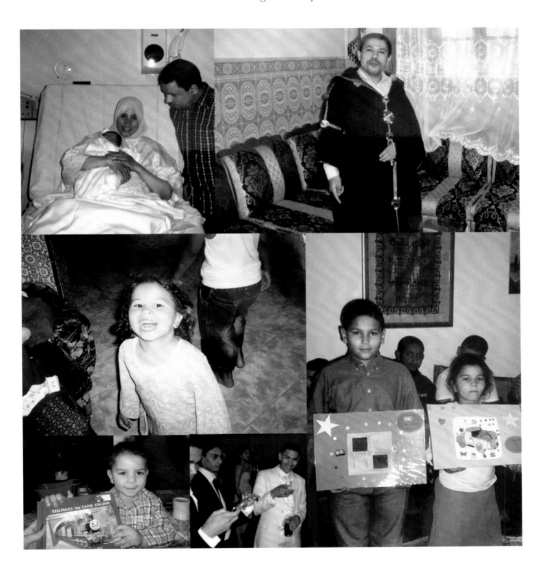

Abdulaziz, El Wahabi   1 December 1964 - 14 June 2017

Faouzia El Wahabi   1 June 1975 - 14 June 2017

Yasin, El Wahabi   9 August 1996 - 14 June 2017

Nur Huda, El Wahabi   27 June 2001 - 14 June 2017

Mehdi El Wahabi   26 February 2009 - 14 June 2017

"You know, the property has no comparison to human life. For me they are things that you can re-buy. The one difficulty and I am not going to lie is photos, because I had photos of my children when they were young, newborn and things like that and you can't get those things back. I am just trying to create new ones now."

- Hanan

IN LOVING MEMORY OF_

Abdeslam Sebbar

Ali Yawar Jafari

Denis Murphy

Mohammed Al-Haj Ali

Jeremiah Deen

Zainab Deen

Steven Power

Sheila

Joe 'Joseph' Daniels

Husna Begum

Kamru Miah

Mohammed Hamid

Mohammed Hanif

Rabeya Begum

Khadija Khaloufi

Vincent Chiejina

Fatemeh Afrasehabi

Sakineh Afrasehabi

Isaac Paulos

Hamid Kani

Berkti Haftom

Biruk Haftom

Gary Maunders

Deborah 'Debbie' Lamprell

Ernie Vital

Marjorie Vital

Maria Del-Pilar Burton

Amal Ahmedin

Amaya Tuccu-Ahmedin

Amna Mahmud Idris

Mohamednur Tuccu

Victoria King

Alexandra Atala

Mary Mendy

Khadija Saye

Ligaya Moore

Jessica Urbano

Farah Hamdan Belkadi

Leena Belkadi

Malak Belkadi

Omar Belkadi

Abdulaziz El Wahabi

Faouzia El-Wahabi

Mehdi El-Wahabi

Nur Huda El Wahabi

Yasin El Wahabi

Logan Gomes

Firdaws Hashim

Hashim Kedir

Nura Jemal

Yahya Hashim

Yaqub Hashim

Fatima Choucair

Mierna Choucair

Nadia Choucair

Sirria Choucair

Zainab Choucair

Bassem Choucair

Anthony 'Tony' Disson

Mariem Elgwahry

Eslah Elgwahry

Raymond 'Moses' Bernard Gloria

Trevisan

Marco Gottardi

Fethia Hassan

Hania Hassan

Rania Ibrahim

Hesham Rahman

Mohamed 'Saber' Amied Neda

Abufras Ibrahim

Isra Ibrahim

Fathia Ali Ahmed Elsanosi

THANK YOU_

I want to thank God for being the source of my strength, courage and inspiration throughout this process and never leaving me. For the hope I have in Jesus, to continue through suffering and the promise of life beyond death. - Revelations 21:4

Thank you to my friends and family for surrounding me these past few years and to everyone who has gotten behind this vision, made contributions and helped make this possible. I am so grateful for every supporter and collaborator near and far.

Afewerki Abraha	Marcus Liberman	Fola Iyiola Soyoye
Fatima Ahmedin	Hannah Burt	Anjola Adelaja
Winta Afewerki	Joseph Daley	Jacob Roberts
Hawa Ahmedin	Thembe Mvula	Yosola Olorunshola
Elena Beyene	Emma Heddle	Andre Anderson
Sofi Samuel	Cath Carter	Ellen Stewart
Yemane Gebreegzuabher	Daniel Renwick	Neelam Keshwala
Kelit Alazar	Michael Perkins	Shareefa Energy
Aida Alazar	Daniel Perkins	Amanda Asare
Yenabi Mezghebe	Reis Morris	Monica Kheir
Selam Ibrahim	Marcia Robinson	Kirsty Totimeh
Sabrina Ibrahim	Kat Sladden	Milka Yemane
Babirye Katende	Rags Martel	Funmi Abari
Isobel Joseph	Raja Chellat	Rhoda Ofori-Attah
Jessica Oomen	Amell El-Guenuni	Deborah Lauder
Jonathan Oomen	Millie Hawley	Fiona Doherty
Esther Koovor	Gabrielle Hamill	Vestalia Chilton
Sarah Morton	Hannah Yongo	Bolanle Tajudeen
Chloe Taylor	Iona Ledwidge	Rebecca Gremmo
Dionne Reid	Kings Cross church	Renay Taylor
Emma Liberman	Harriette Foster	Diane Morgan

SUPPORTERS

Grenfell Foundation	Rugby Portobello Trust	K&C Foundation
Howard Taylor	Mark Simms	Brooke Dobbyn
Tessa Barkhan		Jon Fryer
Ruba Ahmed		

ACKNOWLEDGEMENTS_

CONTRIBUTORS

Ed Daffarn

Shafika Ragab

Mohammed Ragab

Nashwa Maher

Noha El Baghdady

Omar El Baghdady

Zoë Dainton

Andreia Leitao

Rosie Leitao Donnelly

Susan Rudnik

Lucy Knight-Ballard

Leanne & Malachi

Natasha Elcock

Gaby & Esther

Mouna El-Ogbani

Zaid Khalloud

Feruza Afewerki

Fatima Ahmedin

Corinne Jones

Turufat Yilma

Tiago Alves

Bobby Ross

Nadia Aasili

Karim Mussilhy

Vega Nowak

Kai Mussilhy

Maia Mussilhy

David Krome

Tim Downie

Zeyad Cred

Swarzy Macaly

Adele May

Adiam Ekubay

Theo Negussie

Azael Negussie

Sue Duggins

Maxine Duggins

Bellal El Guenuni

Joseph John

Bernadette Bernard

Zoe-Ann Bernard-Panton

Sarah-Jayne Bernard

Hanan Wahabi

Sara Chebiouni

Zak Chebiouni

Sandra Ruiz

THE PRODUCTION TEAM

Magdalene Abraha

Tom Cockram

James Kenny

Saraphina Mattis

Editor

Creative Mentor

Photobook Retoucher

Graphic / Website Design

GOLD & ASHES TEAM_

When beginning this photo book we knew that a project as complex and nuanced as this meant we could never tell the whole story, but the seventy two innocent lives that were lost and the community around them have inspired us to honour and share a part of their stories.

Without the commitment and support of my team, a group of volunteer creatives who brought their hearts and minds in collaborating to create this photo series with me, this photo book would not exist. Each person on this team has devoted their time and energy to sharing the contributions made with so much care and consideration.

Feruza Afewerki	Creative Director / Photographer
Paula Bernal	Graphic Designer
Errol Donald	Creative Consultant
Hermine Kudia	Project Manager
Cheyenne Dwyer-Mcdowall	Social Media Manager
Yetunde Animashaun	Mental Health Co-ordinator
Fauzia Amao	Editor / Copywriter
Marie-Kathrin Blanck	Photographs Curator
Safiya Akinrinlola	Print Producer
Tara Leigh	Creative Planner / Photographer
Zachary Crawley	Candour / Film maker
Ben Saunders	Candour / Film maker